Fun With Words

Animal Antics ABCs

CHATHAM RIVER PRESS
New York

Created and manufactured by arrangement with Ottenheimer Publishers, Inc.
Copyright © 1990 Ottenheimer Publishers, Inc.
This 1990 edition published by Ottenheimer Publishers, Inc.,
for Chatham River Press, a division of Arlington House, Inc.,
distributed by Crown Publishers, Inc., 225 Park Avenue South,
New York, New York 10003
All rights reserved
Printed in Singapore
ISBN 0-517-68881-6
h g f e d c b a

Bb

BIRD

BALLOON

BEAR BITING A BANANA

BIRTHDAY CAKE

BUNNY

BOOTS

BISCUITS

BROOM

BADGER

BLACKBOARD

BIG BONE

BOW

BOY SCOUT

BUGLE

BICYCLE

BRUSH

BATH

BUCKET

BOAT

BIRD HOUSE

BUBBLES

BABY

BALD

BARBER

BAT

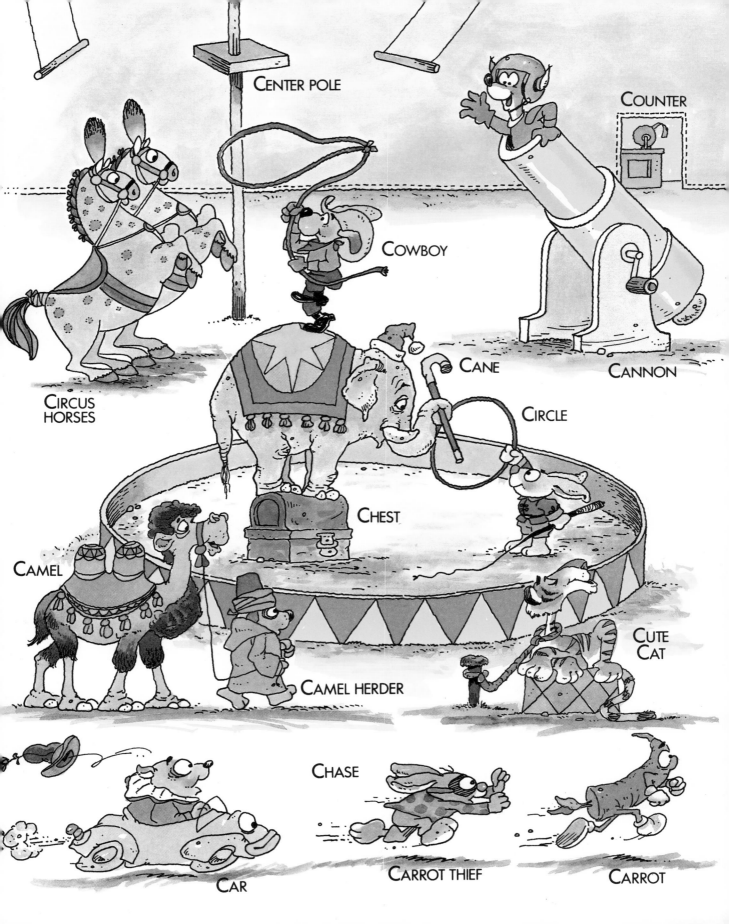

CENTER POLE

COUNTER

COWBOY

CANE

CANNON

CIRCUS HORSES

CIRCLE

CHEST

CAMEL

CUTE CAT

CAMEL HERDER

CHASE

CAR

CARROT THIEF

CARROT

DERBY

DOOR KNOB

DIPLOMA

AT THE DOCTOR

DRINK

DIAPER

DIAPER BAG

DRAWERS

DRESSING

DOLL

DEEP BREATH

DOCTORS

DIET

DAZZLING SMILE

DRESS

DESK

EAGLE

EXCITED

ENGINEER

ELECTRIC TRAIN

EMPTY

EYE

EYEBROW

EYELASH

EYE CHART

EXPLORER

ELECTRICIAN

Gg

GRAPES

GOAT

GLASSES

GORILLA

GLOVES

GOPHER

GUITAR

GATE

GARDEN

GOOSE

GOLF

GRIZZLY BEAR

GRASS

GIRAFFE

GOLD

GHOST

GARBAGE MAN

GARBAGE CAN

GRASSHOPPER

Hh
AT HOME

HELICOPTER

HIPPO

HEDGE

HAMMOCK

HAMSTER

HAT

HAND

HOT DOGS

HAMBURGERS

HOOP

HEN

HOSE

HAMMER

HOUSE

HANGING HIGH

HOT

HIDING

HAMPER

HANGING LAMP

HARRY

HORN

HARMONICA

HAM

HONEY

HADDOCK

HERBS

HASSOCK

Ii

INDIAN

ISLAND

ICE SKATE

IRON

IRONING BOARD

INK

BLACK

ICE CREAM

INSECT

ICE CREAM CONE

IGLOO

INCH WORM

1   2

INCH

Jj

JUNGLE

JACK-O-LANTERN

JAR

JELLYBEANS

JUGGLER

JUDGE

JUMP

JEWEL

JUMP ROPE

JEWELER

KENNEL

GUARD DOG

KICK

KNOT

KNOT TYING PROJECT

KIWI FRUIT

KINDLING WOOD

KEROSENE LAMP

KNAPSACK

KNIFE

KISS

Ll

LIGHTNING BUG

LIGHT BULB

LEOPARD

LADDER

LION

LAUGHING

LAZY LOBSTER

LOG

LANTERN

LIGHTHOUSE

LIFEBOAT

LIZARD

LOLLIPOP

LAWNMOWER

LAWN

LETTER

LASSO

LEAF

LUNCH BOX

LUNCH

LOCK

MUSIC

MARCHING

MANNEQUIN

MACHO MAN'S SHOP

MACHO MAN

MAINTENANCE MAN

MUG

MOP PAIL

MOP

MESS

MODEL

BRIDAL SHOP

MELTING ICE CREAM

MATTRESS

MAIL

MAILMAN

MAILBAG

MITTENS

LOST AND FOUND

SALE

MATTRESS SALE

2ND FLOOR

Oo

OLD MR. OTTER

OVERCOAT

ORGAN

OPEN BOOK

OCTOPUS

OVERCAST

OLIVE

OFF

OCEAN

OAR

OYSTER

OLIVES

OSTRICH

PINE TREES

PLAYGROUND

PLAYGROUND AREA

PANDA

PICNIC

PIE

PITCHER

PAPER CUPS

PENNY

PICKLES

PLATE

PICNIC BASKET

PURSE

PATH

PLAYING

PARK BENCH

PEANUTS

PIGEONS

Qq AT THE RESTAURANT

QUARTER

S-S-SHH

QUESTION

QUAIL

QUICHE

QUIET

QUARTET

QUACK

QUINCE JUICE

QUART

QUEEN

QUOIT

QUILT

NIGHTLY
THE
SINGIN
WAITER

TAXI

TIRE

TREE TRUNK

TOOL CHEST

TOOLS

TENNIS BALL

TENNIS RACQUET

TONGUE

TOY

TRUNK

TATTOO

TELEVISION

TRICYCLE

Uu

Umbrella

Up

Upside-down

Unicorn

Underwear

Unicycle

Underpass

Uniform

Under

Ukulele

VIOLINIST

VIOLIN

Vv

VEHICLE

VETERINARIAN

VIPER

VET

VAN

VISOR

VEGETABLES

VACATION

Ww

WASHING

WHALE

WOODPECKER

WOOD

WAGON

WIG

WALRUS

WING

WATCHING

WORM

Xx

X-RAY

XYLOPHONE

Yy

YO-YO

YAWNING YAK

YARN

Zz

ZINNIAS FOR SALE

ZEBRA

ZIPPER

ZINNIAS